S0-BMV-979

BIBLE
ANSWERS
for the
NEW YEAR

BIBLE
ANSWERS
for the
NEW YEAR

BARBOUR
PUBLISHING

© 2009 by Barbour Publishing, Inc.

ISBN 978-1-60260-384-4

All rights reserved. No part of this publication may be reproduced or transmitted for commercial purposes, except for brief quotations in printed reviews, without written permission of the publisher.

All scripture quotations are taken from the King James Version of the Bible.

Published by Barbour Publishing, Inc., P.O. Box 719, Uhrichsville, Ohio 44683, www.barbourbooks.com

Our mission is to publish and distribute inspirational products offering exceptional value and biblical encouragement to the masses.

 Member of the
Evangelical Christian
Publishers Association

Printed in the United States of America.

INTRODUCTION

Every new year is a time of reflection and questions: How should we approach the future? Why resist temptation? Where can we find true happiness? What is real success?

In His loving-kindness, God has answered all of these questions—and many more—in the pages of His Word, the Bible. Whatever our needs, we can find in scripture every answer we can ask or imagine. This collection of Bible verses is a handy reference for some of the key issues that we all struggle to reconcile—especially at the beginning of the year.

This book is not intended to replace regular, personal Bible study. Nor is it meant to replace a concordance for in-depth study of a particular subject. It is, however, intended to be a quick reference for those seeking inspiration and guidance. We hope it will be a source of encouragement for you now and for many years to come.

THE EDITORS

CONTENTS

ACHIEVING GOALS

Ah, resolution season. Time to shape up, lose weight, kick the habit, and be better. How long will we keep these promises to ourselves this year? A month? A week?

Setting goals is a good way to start every new year, but as important as it is to lay the groundwork, it's even more important to follow through and achieve those goals. This year, don't forget to invite God into your plans. Ask Him for guidance and for strength as you work toward mastering this year's resolutions. If you're acting in His will, He'll help you succeed.

Father, I can't reach my goals on my own.
Please bless the ways I'm trying better myself this year.
Amen.

Brethren, I count not myself to have
apprehended: but this one thing I do, forgetting
those things which are behind, and reaching
forth unto those things which are before, I press
toward the mark for the prize of the high
calling of God in Christ Jesus.

Philippians 3:13–14

He giveth power to the faint; and to them that
have no might he increaseth strength. . . . But
they that wait upon the Lord shall renew their
strength; they shall mount up with wings as
eagles; they shall run, and not be weary;
and they shall walk, and not faint.

Isaiah 40:29, 31

And so, after he had patiently endured,
he obtained the promise.

Hebrews 6:15

I know both how to be abased,
and I know how to abound: every
where and in all things I am instructed
both to be full and to be hungry,
both to abound and to suffer need.
I can do all things through Christ
which strengtheneth me.

Philippians 4:12–13

Jesus said unto him, If thou canst believe,
all things are possible to him that believeth.
MARK 9:23

Watch ye, stand fast in the faith,
quit you like men, be strong.
1 CORINTHIANS 16:13

Thou therefore endure hardness,
as a good soldier of Jesus Christ.
2 TIMOTHY 2:3

Though he fall, he shall not be utterly cast down:
for the LORD upholdeth him with his hand.
PSALM 37:24

Let us lay aside every weight, and the sin which
doth so easily beset us, and let us run with
patience the race that is set before us.
HEBREWS 12:1

Happy is he that hath the God of Jacob for his
help, whose hope is in the LORD his God.
PSALM 146:5

The joy of the LORD is your strength.
NEHEMIAH 8:10

But if thou wilt go, do it, be strong for the
battle: God shall make thee fall before the enemy:
for God hath power to help, and to cast down.
2 CHRONICLES 25:8

But be not thou far from me, O LORD:
O my strength, haste thee to help me.
PSALM 22:19

The thoughts of the diligent tend only
to plenteousness; but of every one
that is hasty only to want.
PROVERBS 21:5

Wherefore the rather, brethren, give diligence
to make your calling and election sure:
for if ye do these things, ye shall never fall.
2 PETER 1:10

Look to yourselves, that we lose not
those things which we have wrought,
but that we receive a full reward.
2 JOHN 1:8

*W*herefore take unto you the
whole armour of God, that ye
may be able to withstand in
the evil day, and having
done all, to stand.

EPHESIANS 6:13

And Jesus looking upon them saith,
With men it is impossible, but not with God:
for with God all things are possible.
Mark 10:27

For thou shalt eat the labour of thine hands:
happy shalt thou be, and it shall
be well with thee.
Psalm 128:2

Whatsoever thy hand findeth to do,
do it with thy might; for there is no work,
nor device, nor knowledge, nor wisdom,
in the grave, whither thou goest.
Ecclesiastes 9:10

ADVERSITY

What mountain are you climbing? From small daily struggles to monumental life-changers, everyone faces adversity. How does God want us to deal with these troubles when they come?

Jesus urges us to put everything in perspective. In John 16:33, He tells us that He knows we're going to have troubles in this world. But look at the bigger picture—even in the middle of troubles, He is still in control and will conquer evil once and for all.

Take comfort in the fact that your Deliverer is coming—and coming soon.

Jesus, You alone can lift the burdens of the struggles I'm facing. I submit them to You and Your will. Amen.

And though the Lord give you the bread of
adversity, and the water of affliction, yet shall
not thy teachers be removed into a corner any
more, but thine eyes shall see thy teachers: and
thine ears shall hear a word behind thee, saying,
This is the way, walk ye in it, when ye turn to the
right hand, and when ye turn to the left.
ISAIAH 30:20–21

The LORD shall fight for you,
and ye shall hold your peace.
EXODUS 14:14

And it shall come to pass in the day that
the LORD shall give thee rest from thy sorrow,
and from thy fear, and from the hard bondage
wherein thou wast made to serve.
ISAIAH 14:3

Verily, verily, I say unto you,
That ye shall weep and lament,
but the world shall rejoice: and ye
shall be sorrowful, but your sorrow
shall be turned into joy.

JOHN 16:20

The righteous cry, and the LORD heareth,
and delivereth them out of all their troubles.
PSALM 34:17

Blessed are ye, when men shall hate you, and
when they shall separate you from their company,
and shall reproach you, and cast out your name
as evil, for the Son of man's sake.
LUKE 6:22

The angel of the LORD encampeth round about
them that fear him, and delivereth them.
PSALM 34:7

For in the time of trouble he shall hide me
in his pavilion: in the secret of his tabernacle
shall he hide me; he shall set me up upon a rock.
And now shall mine head be lifted up above
mine enemies round about me: therefore will I
offer in his tabernacle sacrifices of joy; I will sing,
yea, I will sing praises unto the LORD.
PSALM 27:5–6

Though he fall, he shall not be utterly cast down:
for the LORD upholdeth him with his hand.
PSALM 37:24

For I reckon that the sufferings of this present
time are not worthy to be compared with
the glory which shall be revealed in us.
ROMANS 8:18

He shall cover thee with his feathers, and under
his wings shalt thou trust: his truth shall be thy
shield and buckler. Thou shalt not be afraid for
the terror by night; nor for the arrow that flieth
by day; nor for the pestilence that walketh in
darkness; nor for the destruction that wasteth
at noonday. A thousand shall fall at thy side,
and ten thousand at thy right hand; but
it shall not come nigh thee.
PSALM 91:4–7

For our light affliction, which is but for
a moment, worketh for us a far more
exceeding and eternal weight of glory.
2 CORINTHIANS 4:17

Beloved, think it not strange concerning the
fiery trial which is to try you, as though some
strange thing happened unto you: but rejoice,
inasmuch as ye are partakers of Christ's
sufferings; that, when his glory shall be revealed,
ye may be glad also with exceeding joy.
1 PETER 4:12–13

Peace I leave with you, my peace I give unto you:
not as the world giveth, give I unto you. Let not
your heart be troubled, neither let it be afraid.
JOHN 14:27

Who shall separate us from the love of Christ?
shall tribulation, or distress, or persecution,
or famine, or nakedness, or peril, or sword?
ROMANS 8:35

But if thou shalt indeed obey his voice,
and do all that I speak; then I will be an
enemy unto thine enemies, and an
adversary unto thine adversaries.
EXODUS 23:22

When thou passest through the waters, I will be with thee; and through the rivers, they shall not overflow thee: when thou walkest through the fire, thou shalt not be burned; neither shall the flame kindle upon thee.

ISAIAH 43:2

In God have I put my trust:
I will not be afraid what man can do unto me.
Psalm 56:11

For as the sufferings of Christ abound in us,
so our consolation also aboundeth by Christ.
2 Corinthians 1:5

Fear thou not; for I am with thee: be not
dismayed; for I am thy God: I will strengthen
thee; yea, I will help thee; yea, I will uphold thee
with the right hand of my righteousness.
Isaiah 41:10

ANXIETY ABOUT THE FUTURE

We humans sure do like to have control. But most daily occurrences are out of our hands—so we worry. We lie awake at night worrying about tomorrow. We plan. We scheme. We manipulate to try to make things go the way we want.

God has a better way. He wants us to lay our future at His feet and give it to Him completely—not keeping one scrap in our pockets that we can worry to death.

Enter into the freedom that God's anti-anxiety guarantee offers. Give it all to Him.

Father God, I give my future to You. Lead me on Your right and true path today, tomorrow, and forever. Amen.

Jesus Christ the same yesterday,
and to day, and for ever.
HEBREWS 13:8

For I know the thoughts that I think toward
you, saith the LORD, thoughts of peace, and not
of evil, to give you an expected end.
JEREMIAH 29:11

And the world passeth away, and the
lust thereof: but he that doeth the
will of God abideth for ever.
1 JOHN 2:17

I laid me down and slept; I awaked; for the
LORD sustained me. I will not be afraid
of ten thousands of people, that have set
themselves against me round about.
PSALM 3:5–6

The LORD is my light and my
salvation; whom shall I fear? the
LORD is the strength of my life;
of whom shall I be afraid?

PSALM 27:1

These things I have spoken unto you, that
in me ye might have peace. In the world ye
shall have tribulation: but be of good cheer;
I have overcome the world.

John 16:33

For I am persuaded, that neither death, nor life,
nor angels, nor principalities, nor powers,
nor things present, nor things to come,
nor height, nor depth, nor any other creature,
shall be able to separate us from the love of
God, which is in Christ Jesus our Lord.

Romans 8:38–39

Have not I commanded thee? Be strong and
of a good courage; be not afraid, neither be
thou dismayed: for the Lord thy God is
with thee whithersoever thou goest.

Joshua 1:9

And thou shalt be secure, because there is hope;
yea, thou shalt dig about thee, and thou
shalt take thy rest in safety.

Job 11:18

He shall cover thee with his feathers, and under his wings shalt thou trust: his truth shall be thy shield and buckler. Thou shalt not be afraid for the terror by night; nor for the arrow that flieth by day; nor for the pestilence that walketh in darkness; nor for the destruction that wasteth at noonday. A thousand shall fall at thy side, and ten thousand at thy right hand; but it shall not come nigh thee.

PSALM 91:4–7

Remember therefore how thou hast received and heard, and hold fast, and repent. If therefore thou shalt not watch, I will come on thee as a thief, and thou shalt not know what hour I will come upon thee.

REVELATION 3:3

Though thy beginning was small, yet thy latter end should greatly increase.

JOB 8:7

When thou liest down, thou shalt not
be afraid: yea, thou shalt lie down,
and thy sleep shall be sweet.
PROVERBS 3:24

And God shall wipe away all tears from their
eyes; and there shall be no more death, neither
sorrow, nor crying, neither shall there be any
more pain: for the former things are passed away.
REVELATION 21:4

And, lo, I am with you always,
even unto the end of the world.
MATTHEW 28:20

Be not afraid of sudden fear, neither of the
desolation of the wicked, when it cometh.
For the LORD shall be thy confidence, and
shall keep thy foot from being taken.
PROVERBS 3:25–26

Be patient therefore, brethren, unto the coming of the Lord. Behold, the husbandman waiteth for the precious fruit of the earth, and hath long patience for it, until he receive the early and latter rain. Be ye also patient; stablish your hearts: for the coming of the Lord draweth nigh.

JAMES 5:7–8

*W*ho shall separate us from the love of Christ?
shall tribulation, or distress, or persecution,
or famine, or nakedness, or peril, or sword?
Romans 8:35

*A*gain I say unto you, That if two of you
shall agree on earth as touching any thing
that they shall ask, it shall be done for them
of my Father which is in heaven. For where
two or three are gathered together in my name,
there am I in the midst of them.
Matthew 18:19–20

*G*od is our refuge and strength, a very
present help in trouble. Therefore will not
we fear, though the earth be removed, and
though the mountains be carried into the midst
of the sea; though the waters thereof roar and
be troubled, though the mountains shake
with the swelling thereof.
Psalm 46:1–3

BUILDING RELATIONSHIPS

What relationships do you need to work on this year?

Some relationships are easy, and some take work. But before you write off the difficult ones and decide you can do without those people in your life, consider this: God can be glorified in every relationship, and maybe He's trying to teach you something as you work to strengthen the bonds you have with others.

Give God your relationships and expect the blessings to follow.

Father God, please help me build strong relationships with the people in my life. Help me to show Your love to them. Amen.

Rejoice with them that do rejoice,
and weep with them that weep.
ROMANS 12:15

A friend loveth at all times.
PROVERBS 17:17

Nevertheless, let every one of you in particular
so love his wife even as himself; and the
wife see that she reverence her husband.
EPHESIANS 5:33

Ointment and perfume rejoice the heart:
so doth the sweetness of a man's
friend by hearty counsel.
PROVERBS 27:9

And, ye fathers, provoke not your children to
wrath: but bring them up in the nurture and
admonition of the Lord.
EPHESIANS 6:4

Brethren, if any of you do err from the truth,
and one convert him; let him know, that he
which converteth the sinner from the error
of his way shall save a soul from death,
and shall hide a multitude of sins.
JAMES 5:19–20

Correct thy son, and he shall give thee rest; yea,
he shall give delight unto thy soul.
PROVERBS 29:17

Wherefore comfort yourselves together,
and edify one another, even as also ye do.
1 THESSALONIANS 5:11

Let every one of us please his neighbour
for his good to edification.
ROMANS 15:2

Ye have heard that it hath been said, Thou
shalt love thy neighbour, and hate thine enemy.
But I say unto you, Love your enemies, bless
them that curse you, do good to them that hate
you, and pray for them which despitefully
use you, and persecute you.
MATTHEW 5:43–44

Be kindly affectioned one to another with
brotherly love; in honour preferring one another.
ROMANS 12:10

Confess your faults one to another, and pray one
for another, that ye may be healed. The effectual
fervent prayer of a righteous man availeth much.
JAMES 5:16

Thou shalt not avenge, nor bear any grudge
against the children of thy people, but thou shalt
love thy neighbour as thyself: I am the LORD.
LEVITICUS 19:18

And let us consider one another to
provoke unto love and to good works.
HEBREWS 10:24

Iron sharpeneth iron; so a man sharpeneth
the countenance of his friend.
PROVERBS 27:17

Finally, be ye all of one mind, having
compassion one of another, love as brethren,
be pitiful, be courteous.
1 PETER 3:8

Be of the same mind one toward another.
Mind not high things, but condescend to men
of low estate. Be not wise in your own conceits.
ROMANS 12:16

These are the things that ye shall do; Speak ye
every man the truth to his neighbour; execute
the judgment of truth and peace in your gates.
ZECHARIAH 8:16

*T*hus speaketh the LORD of hosts, saying,
Execute true judgment, and shew mercy and
compassions every man to his brother: and
oppress not the widow, nor the fatherless, the
stranger, nor the poor; and let none of you
imagine evil against his brother in your heart.
ZECHARIAH 7:9–10

*N*ow the God of patience and consolation grant
you to be likeminded one toward another
according to Christ Jesus: that ye may with
one mind and one mouth glorify God,
even the Father of our Lord Jesus Christ.
ROMANS 15:5–6

A man that hath friends must shew himself
friendly: and there is a friend that
sticketh closer than a brother.
PROVERBS 18:24

CELEBRATION

Every milestone, every goal achieved in this new year, will be a cause for celebration. It's exciting to look forward to the benchmarks we will set. This year, as you consider every accomplishment, send the praise heavenward to the Author of every achievement. He's not only helping you along the way, He's on your side, rooting for your every success.

This year will bring many causes for celebration, Lord! I praise You for the works that You will accomplish in my life! Amen.

*B*ehold that which I have seen: it is good
and comely for one to eat and to drink,
and to enjoy the good of all his labour that
he taketh under the sun all the days of his life,
which God giveth him: for it is his portion.
Every man also to whom God hath given riches
and wealth, and hath given him power to eat
thereof, and to take his portion, and to rejoice
in his labour; this is the gift of God.
ECCLESIASTES 5:18–19

*A*nd this day shall be unto you for a memorial;
and ye shall keep it a feast to the LORD
throughout your generations; ye shall keep
it a feast by an ordinance for ever.
EXODUS 12:14

*A*nd bring hither the fatted calf, and kill it;
and let us eat, and be merry.
LUKE 15:23

*M*ake a joyful noise unto the Lord,
all the earth: make a loud noise,
and rejoice, and sing praise.

PSALM 98:4

And ye shall eat in plenty, and be satisfied,
and praise the name of the Lord your God,
that hath dealt wondrously with you.
Joel 2:26

Let the heavens rejoice, and let the earth be glad;
let the sea roar, and the fulness thereof.
Let the field be joyful, and all that is therein:
then shall all the trees of the wood rejoice.
Psalm 96:11–12

Rejoice in the Lord always: and again I say,
Rejoice.
Philippians 4:4

Let them praise his name in the dance: let them
sing praises unto him with the timbrel and harp.
Psalm 149:3

The LORD reigneth; let the earth rejoice;
let the multitude of isles be glad thereof.
PSALM 97:1

Go thy way, eat thy bread with joy,
and drink thy wine with a merry heart;
for God now accepteth thy works.
ECCLESIASTES 9:7

Serve the LORD with fear,
and rejoice with trembling.
PSALM 2:11

And thou shalt rejoice in thy feast, thou,
and thy son, and thy daughter, and thy
manservant, and thy maidservant, and the
Levite, the stranger, and the fatherless,
and the widow, that are within thy gates.
DEUTERONOMY 16:14

And all the people went their way to eat,
and to drink, and to send portions, and to
make great mirth, because they had understood
the words that were declared unto them.
NEHEMIAH 8:12

Let us walk honestly, as in the day; not in rioting
and drunkenness, not in chambering and
wantonness, not in strife and envying.
ROMANS 13:13

Drunkenness, revellings, and such like: of
the which I tell you before, as I have also told
you in time past, that they which do such
things shall not inherit the kingdom of God.
GALATIANS 5:21

For thou shalt eat the labor of thine hands:
happy shalt thou be, and it shall be
well with thee.
PSALM 128:2

And there ye shall eat before the
LORD your God, and ye shall rejoice
in all that ye put your hand unto, ye
and your households, wherein the
LORD thy God hath blessed thee.

DEUTERONOMY 12:7

*T*his is the day which the LORD hath made;
we will rejoice and be glad in it.
PSALM 118:24

*A*nd take thou unto thee of all food that is eaten,
and thou shalt gather it to thee; and it shall
be for food for thee, and for them.
GENESIS 6:21

*M*y lips shall greatly rejoice when I sing unto
thee; and my soul, which thou hast redeemed.
PSALM 71:23

FINDING PEACE

Peace is one of those ellusive goals that everyone strives for, but few achieve. Part of the problem is that the world is much too loud—headlines screaming, gossip shouting, problems screeching.

So if you're looking for peace in this new year, start by opening up the Word. Soon you'll hear more of the Father's voice and less of the noise of the world. Then converse with Him in prayer. Be still and experience the joy of God's peace.

Almighty God, show me how to better live in You, so that I can experience Your peace to the fullest. Amen.

These things I have spoken unto you,
that in me ye might have peace. In the world
ye shall have tribulation: but be of good
cheer; I have overcome the world.
John 16:33

Is any among you afflicted? let him pray.
James 5:13

Come unto me, all ye that labour and are heavy
laden, and I will give you rest.
Matthew 11:28

I exhort therefore, that, first
of all, supplications, prayers,
intercessions, and giving of thanks,
be made for all men; for kings, and
for all that are in authority; that we
may lead a quiet and peaceable life
in all godliness and honesty.

1 TIMOTHY 2:1–2

But the meek shall inherit the earth; and shall
delight themselves in the abundance of peace.
PSALM 37:11

Be perfect, be of good comfort, be of one mind,
live in peace; and the God of love and
peace shall be with you.
2 CORINTHIANS 13:11

And the fruit of righteousness is sown
in peace of them that make peace.
JAMES 3:18

Behold, how good and how pleasant it is
for brethren to dwell together in unity!
PSALM 133:1

For he that will love life, and see good days,
let him refrain his tongue from evil, and his lips
that they speak no guile: let him eschew evil,
and do good; let him seek peace, and ensue it.
1 PETER 3:10–11

Depart from evil, and do good;
seek peace, and pursue it.
PSALM 34:14

Those things, which ye have both learned,
and received, and heard, and seen in me, do:
and the God of peace shall be with you.
PHILIPPIANS 4:9

Study to shew thyself approved unto God,
a workman that needeth not to be ashamed,
rightly dividing the word of truth.
2 TIMOTHY 2:15

I will both lay me down in peace, and sleep:
for thou, LORD, only makest me dwell in safety.
PSALM 4:8

Peace I leave with you, my peace I give unto you:
not as the world giveth, give I unto you. Let not
your heart be troubled, neither let it be afraid.
JOHN 14:27

The mountains shall bring peace to the people,
and the little hills, by righteousness.
PSALM 72:3

Great peace have they which love thy law:
and nothing shall offend them.
PSALM 119:165

The LORD is my shepherd; I shall
not want. He maketh me to lie down
in green pastures: he leadeth me
beside the still waters. He restoreth
my soul: he leadeth me in the paths
of righteousness for his name's sake.
Yea, though I walk through the valley
of the shadow of death, I will fear no
evil: for thou art with me; thy rod
and thy staff they comfort me.

PSALM 23:1–4

Salt is good: but if the salt have lost his
saltness, wherewith will ye season it? Have salt in
yourselves, and have peace one with another.
MARK 9:50

For to be carnally minded is death; but to be
spiritually minded is life and peace.
ROMANS 8:6

Acquaint now thyself with him, and be at peace:
thereby good shall come unto thee.
JOB 22:21

GIVING TO OTHERS

The world is full of needs. Hunger, disease, and poverty exist halfway around the globe and halfway around the block. Natural disasters create immediate needs—sometimes for thousands of people—in just a few hours of chaos.

Seeing so much need can leave us feeling overwhelmed and hopeless, but God has a better plan. Giving doesn't have to cost much. For a thirsty person, the gift of a cup of water is priceless. And Jesus promises us that when we provide for those in need, we're showing our love for Him (Matthew 25:40).

Jesus, thank You for the privilege of giving to others in Your name. Help me to always answer the call. Amen.

Charity suffereth long, and is kind;
charity envieth not; charity vaunteth not itself,
is not puffed up, doth not behave itself unseemly,
seeketh not her own, is not easily provoked,
thinketh no evil.

1 Corinthians 13:4–5

Blessed is he that considereth the poor:
the Lord will deliver him in time of trouble.

Psalm 41:1

Therefore if thine enemy hunger, feed him;
if he thirst, give him drink: for in so doing
thou shalt heap coals of fire on his head. Be not
overcome of evil, but overcome evil with good.

Romans 12:20–21

Give, and it shall be given unto you; good
measure, pressed down, and shaken together,
and running over, shall men give into your
bosom. For with the same measure that ye mete
withal it shall be measured to you again.

Luke 6:38

Therefore when thou doest thine alms, do not sound a trumpet before thee, as the hypocrites do in the synagogues and in the streets, that they may have glory of men. Verily I say unto you, They have their reward. But when thou doest alms, let not thy left hand know what thy right hand doeth: that thine alms may be in secret: and thy Father which seeth in secret himself shall reward thee openly.

MATTHEW 6:2–4

For the poor shall never cease out of the land:
therefore I command thee, saying, Thou shalt
open thine hand wide unto thy brother,
to thy poor, and to thy needy, in thy land.
Deuteronomy 15:11

And he saw also a certain poor widow
casting in thither two mites. And he said,
Of a truth I say unto you, that this poor widow
hath cast in more than they all: for all these have
of their abundance cast in unto the offerings
of God: but she of her penury hath cast in
all the living that she had.
Luke 21:2–4

Every man according as he purposeth in his
heart, so let him give; not grudgingly, or of
necessity: for God loveth a cheerful giver.
2 Corinthians 9:7

Be not forgetful to entertain strangers: for
thereby some have entertained angels unawares.
Hebrews 13:2

And thou shalt not glean thy vineyard, neither
shalt thou gather every grape of thy vineyard;
thou shalt leave them for the poor and stranger:
I am the LORD your God.
LEVITICUS 19:10

But when thou makest a feast, call the poor,
the maimed, the lame, the blind: and thou
shalt be blessed; for they cannot recompense
thee: for thou shalt be recompensed at
the resurrection of the just.
LUKE 14:13–14

But if any provide not for his own, and specially
for those of his own house, he hath denied
the faith, and is worse than an infidel.
1 TIMOTHY 5:8

And let us not be weary in well doing:
for in due season we shall reap, if we faint not.
GALATIANS 6:9

And if thy brother be waxen poor, and fallen
in decay with thee; then thou shalt relieve him:
yea, though he be a stranger, or a sojourner;
that he may live with thee.
LEVITICUS 25:35

If a brother or sister be naked, and
destitute of daily food, and one of you say
unto them, Depart in peace, be ye warmed
and filled; notwithstanding ye give them not
those things which are needful to the body;
what doth it profit?
JAMES 2:15–16

Neither do men light a candle, and put it
under a bushel, but on a candlestick; and
it giveth light unto all that are in the house.
Let your light so shine before men, that they
may see your good works, and glorify
your Father which is in heaven.
MATTHEW 5:15–16

And above all things have fervent charity among
yourselves: for charity shall cover the multitude
of sins. Use hospitality one to another without
grudging. As every man hath received the gift,
even so minister the same one to another, as good
stewards of the manifold grace of God.

1 PETER 4:8–10

For I was an hungred, and ye gave me meat:
I was thirsty, and ye gave me drink: I was a
stranger, and ye took me in: naked, and ye
clothed me: I was sick, and ye visited me: I was
in prison, and ye came unto me. Then shall the
righteous answer him, saying, Lord, when saw
we thee an hungred, and fed thee? or thirsty, and
gave thee drink? When saw we thee a stranger,
and took thee in? or naked, and clothed thee? Or
when saw we thee sick, or in prison, and came
unto thee? And the King shall answer and say
unto them, Verily I say unto you, Inasmuch as ye
have done it unto one of the least of these
my brethren, ye have done it unto me.

MATTHEW 25:35–40

*T*hough I speak with the tongues of men and
of angels, and have not charity, I am become
as sounding brass, or a tinkling cymbal.
And though I have the gift of prophecy, and
understand all mysteries, and all knowledge; and
though I have all faith, so that I could remove
mountains, and have not charity, I am nothing.
And though I bestow all my goods to feed the
poor, and though I give my body to be burned,
and have not charity, it profiteth me nothing. . . .
And now abideth faith, hope, charity, these three;
but the greatest of these is charity.
1 CORINTHIANS 13:1–3, 13

*A*nd thou shalt rejoice in thy feast, thou,
and thy son, and thy daughter, and thy
manservant, and thy maidservant, and the
Levite, the stranger, and the fatherless,
and the widow, that are within thy gates.
DEUTERONOMY 16:14

GOD'S PROVISION

God will take care of our needs. Jesus said so in Matthew 6:25–34.

But our Father provides much more than the food we eat and the clothes we wear. He's the Author of the unexpected friendship we need during a rough patch. He makes sure the note of encouragement written by a friend comes just when we need a bit of refreshment. He's the reason the paycheck stretches further than ever before to cover an unexpected bill.

All these things—and more—are how God provides for us. Rest in His strong, giving arms today.

Father, thank You for providing for all my needs—even the ones I don't know about. Amen.

Blessed be the LORD, that hath given rest
unto his people Israel, according to all that he
promised: there hath not failed one word of
all his good promise, which he promised
by the hand of Moses his servant.
1 KINGS 8:56

I will not leave you comfortless:
I will come to you.
JOHN 14:18

And it shall come to pass, when I bring a cloud
over the earth, that the bow shall be seen in the
cloud: and I will remember my covenant, which
is between me and you and every living creature
of all flesh; and the waters shall no more
become a flood to destroy all flesh.
GENESIS 9:14–15

When a man's ways please the LORD,
he maketh even his enemies to
be at peace with him.
PROVERBS 16:7

And it shall come to pass, if thou shalt
hearken diligently unto the voice of the
LORD thy God, to observe and to do all his
commandments which I command thee this
day, that the LORD thy God will set thee on
high above all nations of the earth.
DEUTERONOMY 28:1

If they obey and serve him, they shall spend their
days in prosperity, and their years in pleasures.
JOB 36:11

He shall feed his flock like a shepherd:
he shall gather the lambs with his arm,
and carry them in his bosom, and shall
gently lead those that are with young.
ISAIAH 40:11

The young lions do lack, and suffer hunger:
but they that seek the LORD shall not
want any good thing.
PSALM 34:10

*A*sk, and it shall be given you; seek,
and ye shall find; knock, and it shall be opened
unto you: for every one that asketh receiveth;
and he that seeketh findeth; and to him that
knocketh it shall be opened.

MATTHEW 7:7–8

*N*ow no chastening for the present seemeth to be
joyous, but grievous: nevertheless afterward it
yieldeth the peaceable fruit of righteousness
unto them which are exercised thereby.

HEBREWS 12:11

*A*nd I give unto them eternal life; and they
shall never perish, neither shall any man
pluck them out of my hand.

JOHN 10:28

*F*or by grace are ye saved through faith;
and that not of yourselves: it is the gift of God.

EPHESIANS 2:8

If my people, which are called by my name, shall humble themselves, and pray, and seek my face, and turn from their wicked ways; then will I hear from heaven, and will forgive their sin, and will heal their land.

2 CHRONICLES 7:14

And, behold, I am with thee, and will keep thee in all places whither thou goest, and will bring thee again into this land; for I will not leave thee, until I have done that which I have spoken to thee of.

GENESIS 28:15

Delight thyself also in the LORD; and he shall give thee the desires of thine heart.

PSALM 37:4

If any of thine be driven out unto the outmost parts of heaven, from thence will the LORD thy God gather thee, and from thence will he fetch thee.

DEUTERONOMY 30:4

But, beloved, be not ignorant of this one thing,
that one day is with the Lord as a thousand years,
and a thousand years as one day. The Lord is
not slack concerning his promise, as some men
count slackness; but is longsuffering to us-ward,
not willing that any should perish, but
that all should come to repentance.
2 PETER 3:8–9

If we believe not, yet he abideth faithful:
he cannot deny himself.
2 TIMOTHY 2:13

The LORD shall preserve thee from all evil:
he shall preserve thy soul. The LORD shall
preserve thy going out and thy coming in from
this time forth, and even for evermore.
PSALM 121:7–8

He will not suffer thy foot to be moved: he that
keepeth thee will not slumber. Behold, he that
keepeth Israel shall neither slumber nor sleep.
PSALM 121:3–4

Happiness

Infusing happiness into your life may sound like a tall order. The world tells us that happiness comes from getting more—more money, more toys, more esteem. These pursuits unashamedly promote self, but God's Word tells us that true happiness is found in investing in others.

This year, instead of focusing on pleasing yourself, try investing your time and talents into others. Soon your selfish, worldly desires will melt away and you'll be left with simple, God-given happiness.

Father, please show me ways I can serve others so I can find true heavenly happiness. Amen.

If ye keep my commandments, ye shall
abide in my love; even as I have kept my
Father's commandments, and abide in his
love. These things have I spoken unto you,
that my joy might remain in you, and
that your joy might be full.

JOHN 15:10–11

He that despiseth his neighbour sinneth:
but he that hath mercy on the poor, happy is he.

PROVERBS 14:21

Lo, children are an heritage of the LORD: and
the fruit of the womb is his reward. As arrows are
in the hand of a mighty man; so are children of
the youth. Happy is the man that hath his quiver
full of them: they shall not be ashamed, but they
shall speak with the enemies in the gate.

PSALM 127:3–5

There is nothing better for a man, than that he should eat and drink, and that he should make his soul enjoy good in his labour. This also I saw, that it was from the hand of God. . . . For God giveth to a man that is good in his sight wisdom, and knowledge, and joy: but to the sinner he giveth travail, to gather and to heap up.

ECCLESIASTES 2:24, 26

For we brought nothing into this world, and it
is certain we can carry nothing out. And having
food and raiment let us be therewith content.
1 Timothy 6:7–8

Serve the Lord with gladness:
come before his presence with singing.
Psalm 100:2

Behold, happy is the man whom God
correcteth: therefore despise not thou
the chastening of the Almighty.
Job 5:17

For where your treasure is,
there will your heart be also.
Luke 12:34

Let your conversation be without covetousness;
and be content with such things as ye have:
for he hath said, I will never leave thee,
nor forsake thee.
HEBREWS 13:5

For the kingdom of God is not meat
and drink; but righteousness, and peace,
and joy in the Holy Ghost.
ROMANS 14:17

Happy is that people, that is in such a case: yea,
happy is that people, whose God is the LORD.
PSALM 144:15

All the days of the afflicted are evil: but he
that is of a merry heart hath a continual feast.
PROVERBS 15:15

Thou lovest righteousness, and hatest
wickedness: therefore God, thy God,
hath anointed thee with the oil of
gladness above thy fellows.
Psalm 45:7

Delight thyself also in the Lord;
and he shall give thee the desires of thine heart.
Psalm 37:4

Therefore with joy shall ye draw
water out of the wells of salvation.
Isaiah 12:3

Happy is he that hath the God of Jacob for his
help, whose hope is in the Lord his God.
Psalm 146:5

*B*lessed is every one that feareth the LORD; that walketh in his ways. For thou shalt eat the labour of thine hands: happy shalt thou be, and it shall be well with thee. Thy wife shall be as a fruitful vine by the sides of thine house: thy children like olive plants round about thy table.

PSALM 128:1–3

*T*herefore the redeemed of the LORD shall
return, and come with singing unto Zion; and
everlasting joy shall be upon their head:
they shall obtain gladness and joy; and sorrow
and mourning shall flee away.

ISAIAH 51:11

*B*ut let all those that put their trust in
thee rejoice: let them ever shout for joy,
because thou defendest them: let them also
that love thy name be joyful in thee.

PSALM 5:11

HAVING FAITH

Faith in an all-loving, all-powerful God is a simple feat when times are good, but what about when storms come?

God provides times of smooth sailing so we can strengthen our faith in anticipation of turbulent seas. How, you ask? By digging deep into His Word. By spending quiet time in prayer, listening for His voice. By strengthening friendships with like-minded Christians who will be there when the going gets tough. By worshipping His holy name for the great things He does.

Fortify your faith, and with your Father's help, you'll weather the storm and come out even stronger on the other side.

God, this year I want my faith to grow, to become even stronger. Please help me remain committed to the task.
Amen.

For I am persuaded, that neither death, nor
life, nor angels, nor principalities, nor powers,
nor things present, nor things to come, nor
height, nor depth, nor any other creature,
shall be able to separate us from the love of
God, which is in Christ Jesus our Lord.
ROMANS 8:38–39

And when they bring you unto the synagogues,
and unto magistrates, and powers, take ye no
thought how or what thing ye shall answer, or
what ye shall say: for the Holy Ghost shall teach
you in the same hour what ye ought to say.
LUKE 12:11–12

For we know that if our earthly house
of this tabernacle were dissolved, we have
a building of God, an house not made
with hands, eternal in the heavens.
2 CORINTHIANS 5:1

And Jesus answering saith unto them, Have faith in God. For verily I say unto you, That whosoever shall say unto this mountain, Be thou removed, and be thou cast into the sea; and shall not doubt in his heart, but shall believe that those things which he saith shall come to pass; he shall have whatsoever he saith.

MARK 11:22–23

If thou shalt confess with thy mouth
the Lord Jesus, and shalt believe in thine
heart that God hath raised him from
the dead, thou shalt be saved.
ROMANS 10:9

And the Lord said, If ye had faith as a grain of
mustard seed, ye might say unto this sycamine
tree, Be thou plucked up by the root, and be
thou planted in the sea; and it should obey you.
LUKE 17:6

Now faith is the substance of things hoped for,
the evidence of things not seen.
HEBREWS 11:1

Believe in the LORD your God,
so shall ye be established; believe his
prophets, so shall ye prosper.
2 CHRONICLES 20:20

For we are saved by hope: but hope that is seen is not hope: for what a man seeth, why doth he yet hope for? But if we hope for that we see not, then do we with patience wait for it.
Romans 8:24–25

The Lord is good, a strong hold in the day of trouble; and he knoweth them that trust in him.
Nahum 1:7

Who shall separate us from the love of Christ? shall tribulation, or distress, or persecution, or famine, or nakedness, or peril, or sword?
Romans 8:35

Now no chastening for the present seemeth to be joyous, but grievous: nevertheless afterward it yieldeth the peaceable fruit of righteousness unto them which are exercised thereby.
Hebrews 12:11

The LORD is my rock, and my fortress,
and my deliverer; my God, my strength,
in whom I will trust; my buckler, and the
horn of my salvation, and my high tower.
PSALM 18:2

Therefore, my beloved brethren, be ye
stedfast, unmoveable, always abounding in
the work of the Lord, forasmuch as ye know
that your labour is not in vain in the Lord.
1 CORINTHIANS 15:58

For we walk by faith, not by sight.
2 CORINTHIANS 5:7

Ask in faith, nothing wavering. For he
that wavereth is like a wave of the sea
driven with the wind and tossed.
JAMES 1:6

That Christ may dwell in your hearts
by faith; that ye, being rooted and
grounded in love, may be able to
comprehend with all saints what is
the breadth, and length, and depth,
and height; and to know the love
of Christ, which passeth knowledge,
that ye might be filled with all
the fulness of God.

EPHESIANS 3:17–19

Be thou faithful unto death,
and I will give thee a crown of life.
REVELATION 2:10

Pray without ceasing.
1 THESSALONIANS 5:17

Then shall ye call upon me, and ye shall go and
pray unto me, and I will hearken unto you.
And ye shall seek me, and find me, when ye
shall search for me with all your heart.
JEREMIAH 29:12–13

HEALTH AND WELLNESS

Scripture tells us our bodies are temples of the Lord, but at this time of year, it can be hard to identify ourselves as anything but slaves to the food pyramid.

Though a healthy lifestyle is important, when our perceptions of health are confined to just our physical condition, it becomes easy to underestimate the importance of our spiritual well-being. Begin each day with a prayer, asking God to help you keep your priorities straight. You'll find that when you supplement your daily routine with the Fruits of the Spirit, you and your faith will grow stronger.

Dear Lord, help me stay healthy in body and spirit this year. May I honor You in all I do. Amen.

But they that wait upon the LORD shall renew
their strength; they shall mount up with wings
as eagles; they shall run, and not be weary;
and they shall walk, and not faint.
ISAIAH 40:31

The heart of the wise teacheth his mouth,
and addeth learning to his lips. Pleasant words
are as an honeycomb, sweet to the soul,
and health to the bones.
PROVERBS 16:23–24

Why art thou cast down, O my soul? and why
art thou disquieted within me? hope thou in
God: for I shall yet praise him, who is the health
of my countenance, and my God.
PSALM 42:11

Is any sick among you? let him call for the elders of the church; and let them pray over him, anointing him with oil in the name of the Lord: and the prayer of faith shall save the sick, and the Lord shall raise him up; and if he have committed sins, they shall be forgiven him.

JAMES 5:14–15

The light of the eyes rejoiceth the heart:
and a good report maketh the bones fat.
PROVERBS 15:30

Then shall thy light break forth as the morning,
and thine health shall spring forth speedily:
and thy righteousness shall go before thee;
the glory of the LORD shall be thy reward.
ISAIAH 58:8

For I will restore health unto thee, and I will
heal thee of thy wounds, saith the LORD;
because they called thee an Outcast, saying,
This is Zion, whom no man seeketh after.
JEREMIAH 30:17

A merry heart doeth good like a medicine:
but a broken spirit drieth the bones.
PROVERBS 17:22

Be not wise in thine own eyes: fear the LORD,
and depart from evil. It shall be health to thy
navel, and marrow to thy bones. Honour the
LORD with thy substance, and with the
firstfruits of all thine increase.
PROVERBS 3:7–9

There is that speaketh like the piercings of a
sword: but the tongue of the wise is health.
PROVERBS 12:18

My flesh and my heart faileth: but God is the
strength of my heart, and my portion for ever.
PSALM 73:26

Beloved, I wish above all things that
thou mayest prosper and be in health,
even as thy soul prospereth.
3 JOHN 1:2

And ye shall serve the LORD your God, and he
shall bless thy bread, and thy water; and I will
take sickness away from the midst of thee.
EXODUS 23:25

Woe is me for my hurt! my wound is grievous:
but I said, Truly this is a grief, and I must bear it.
JEREMIAH 10:19

There is no soundness in my flesh because
of thine anger; neither is there any rest
in my bones because of my sin.
PSALM 38:3

Exercise thyself rather unto godliness. For bodily
exercise profiteth little: but godliness is profitable
unto all things, having promise of the life that
now is, and of that which is to come.
1 TIMOTHY 4:7–8

If thou wilt diligently hearken to the voice of the LORD thy God, and wilt do that which is right in his sight, and wilt give ear to his commandments, and keep all his statutes, I will put none of these diseases upon thee, which I have brought upon the Egyptians: for I am the LORD that healeth thee.

EXODUS 15:26

And he shall be unto thee a restorer of thy life,
and a nourisher of thine old age.
Ruth 4:15

Behold, I will bring it health and cure,
and I will cure them, and will reveal unto
them the abundance of peace and truth.
Jeremiah 33:6

And even to your old age I am he; and even to
hoar hairs will I carry you: I have made, and I
will bear; even I will carry, and will deliver you.
Isaiah 46:4

HOPE

There are many New Year traditions that are said to bring good luck and prosperity—sharing a plate of sauerkraut or kissing a sweetheart at midnight, just to name two—but the best way to ring in the New Year is to place your hope in God and trust Him above all else. No amount of sauerkraut can give us confidence in the future like our faith in the Lord can, so whatever your hopes are for the year ahead, keep your heart open to Him and His will for your life. He will never forsake you.

Heavenly Father, I'm looking forward to so much this year. No matter what, I trust that You will guide me down the right path. Amen.

*B*ut let us, who are of the day, be sober,
putting on the breastplate of faith and love;
and for an helmet, the hope of salvation.
1 THESSALONIANS 5:8

*W*herefore gird up the loins of your mind,
be sober, and hope to the end for the grace
that is to be brought unto you at the
revelation of Jesus Christ.
1 PETER 1:13

*W*e glory in tribulations also: knowing that
tribulation worketh patience; and patience,
experience; and experience, hope: and hope
maketh not ashamed; because the love of God
is shed abroad in our hearts by the Holy Ghost
which is given unto us.
ROMANS 5:3–5

Blessed be the God and Father
of our Lord Jesus Christ, which
according to his abundant mercy hath
begotten us again unto a lively hope
by the resurrection of Jesus Christ
from the dead, to an inheritance
incorruptible, and undefiled, and that
fadeth not away, reserved in heaven
for you, who are kept by the power
of God through faith unto salvation
ready to be revealed in the last time.

1 PETER 1:3–5

Therefore my heart is glad, and my glory
rejoiceth: my flesh also shall rest in hope.
PSALM 16:9

Nevertheless we, according to his promise,
look for new heavens and a new earth,
wherein dwelleth righteousness.
2 PETER 3:13

Behold, the eye of the LORD is upon them that
fear him, upon them that hope in his mercy.
PSALM 33:18

But sanctify the Lord God in your hearts:
and be ready always to give an answer to
every man that asketh you a reason of the hope
that is in you with meekness and fear.
1 PETER 3:15

Thou art my hiding place and my shield:
I hope in thy word.
PSALM 119:114

Blessed is the man that trusteth in the LORD,
and whose hope the LORD is.
JEREMIAH 17:7

For we are saved by hope: but hope that is seen
is not hope: for what a man seeth, why doth he
yet hope for? But if we hope for that we see not,
then do we with patience wait for it.
ROMANS 8:24–25

Uphold me according unto thy word, that I may
live: and let me not be ashamed of my hope.
PSALM 119:116

Now the God of hope fill you with all joy and
peace in believing, that ye may abound in
hope, through the power of the Holy Ghost.
Romans 15:13

It is good that a man should both hope and
quietly wait for the salvation of the Lord.
Lamentations 3:26

The Lord taketh pleasure in them that fear
him, in those that hope in his mercy.
Psalm 147:11

And thou shalt be secure, because there is
hope; yea, thou shalt dig about thee,
and thou shalt take thy rest in safety.
Job 11:18

It is of the LORD's mercies
that we are not consumed, because
his compassions fail not. They
are new every morning: great is
thy faithfulness. The LORD is
my portion, saith my soul;
therefore will I hope in him.
LAMENTATIONS 3:22–24

And I give unto them eternal life;
and they shall never perish, neither shall
any man pluck them out of my hand.
JOHN 10:28

But I will hope continually, and will
yet praise thee more and more.
PSALM 71:14

For the law made nothing perfect, but the
bringing in of a better hope did; by the
which we draw nigh unto God.
HEBREWS 7:19

MEASURING SUCCESS

Five. . .four. . .three. . .two. . . one. . . !

The final countdown is an iconic part of
New Year tradition—and the annual flurry of
year-end "top ten" lists has almost become just as
legendary, counting down everything from the
best-dressed celebrity to the businessman with
the biggest bank account.

Though year-end lists can be a fun tribute to
the New Year, as we evaluate and reflect upon our
own lives, it's important that we aren't misled by
false standards of success and happiness. Instead
of fame and fortune, God encourages us to count
the riches of faith, family, love, and generosity as
our greatest treasures.

*God, thank You for all the richness You have brought
into my life. I would have nothing without You. Amen.*

Love not the world, neither the things that
are in the world. If any man love the world,
the love of the Father is not in him.
1 JOHN 2:15

And he said unto his disciples, Therefore I say
unto you, Take no thought for your life, what ye
shall eat; neither for the body, what ye shall put
on. The life is more than meat, and the body is
more than raiment. Consider the ravens: for
they neither sow nor reap; which neither have
storehouse nor barn; and God feedeth them:
how much more are ye better than the fowls?
LUKE 12:22–24

A good name is rather to be chosen
than great riches, and loving favour
rather than silver and gold.
PROVERBS 22:1

Charge them that are rich in this world, that they be not highminded, nor trust in uncertain riches, but in the living God, who giveth us richly all things to enjoy; that they do good, that they be rich in good works, ready to distribute, willing to communicate; laying up in store for themselves a good foundation against the time to come, that they may lay hold on eternal life.

1 Timothy 6:17–19

Labour not for the meat which perisheth,
but for that meat which endureth unto
everlasting life, which the Son of man shall give
unto you: for him hath God the Father sealed.
John 6:27

Therefore, my beloved brethren, be ye stedfast,
unmoveable, always abounding in the work
of the Lord, forasmuch as ye know that your
labour is not in vain in the Lord.
1 Corinthians 15:58

A faithful man shall abound with blessings:
but he that maketh haste to be rich
shall not be innocent.
Proverbs 28:20

He that loveth silver shall not be satisfied
with silver; nor he that loveth abundance
with increase: this is also vanity.
Ecclesiastes 5:10

And why take ye thought for raiment? Consider
the lilies of the field, how they grow; they toil
not, neither do they spin: and yet I say unto you,
That even Solomon in all his glory was not
arrayed like one of these.
MATTHEW 6:28–29

He that tilleth his land shall be satisfied
with bread: but he that followeth vain
persons is void of understanding.
PROVERBS 12:11

Sell that ye have, and give alms; provide
yourselves bags which wax not old, a treasure
in the heavens that faileth not, where no thief
approacheth, neither moth corrupteth. For where
your treasure is, there will your heart be also.
LUKE 12:33–34

Seek ye first the kingdom of God,
and his righteousness; and all these
things shall be added unto you.
MATTHEW 6:33

If a man beget an hundred children,
and live many years, so that the days of his
years be many, and his soul be not filled with
good, and also that he have no burial; I say,
that an untimely birth is better than he.
ECCLESIASTES 6:3

Happy is the man that findeth wisdom, and
the man that getteth understanding. For the
merchandise of it is better than the merchandise
of silver, and the gain thereof than fine gold. She is
more precious than rubies: and all the things thou
canst desire are not to be compared unto her.
PROVERBS 3:13–15

If riches increase, set not your heart upon them.
PSALM 62:10

For wisdom is a defence, and money is a
defence: but the excellency of knowledge is,
that wisdom giveth life to them that have it.
ECCLESIASTES 7:12

*A*nd God said to Solomon,
Because this was in thine heart,
and thou hast not asked riches,
wealth, or honour, nor the life of
thine enemies, neither yet hast asked
long life; but hast asked wisdom and
knowledge for thyself. . .wisdom and
knowledge is granted unto thee.

2 CHRONICLES 1:11-12

They that trust in their wealth, and boast
themselves in the multitude of their riches;
none of them can by any means redeem his
brother, nor give to God a ransom for him:
(for the redemption of their soul is
precious, and it ceaseth for ever).
Psalm 49:6–8

But this I say, He which soweth sparingly shall
reap also sparingly; and he which soweth
bountifully shall reap also bountifully.
2 Corinthians 9:6

A man to whom God hath given riches, wealth,
and honour, so that he wanteth nothing for his
soul of all that he desireth, yet God giveth him
not power to eat thereof, but a stranger eateth it:
this is vanity, and it is an evil disease.
Ecclesiastes 6:2

PATIENCE

As you look ahead to the new year, there are probably only a handful of special days that you're really anticipating: a holiday celebration, a wedding, the birth of child, a retirement, or a long-awaited vacation. It's easy to grow impatient and want to rush through life and wish all the ordinary days away, but even the dullest and most tedious days are precious gifts from the Lord, and He desires that we make the most of each and every one.

So slow down and learn to live one day at a time. It will bring God's plan for your life into perspective and make those special days seem even sweeter.

Lord, I want to make the most of the time You've given me. Help me find purpose in every day. Amen.

*A*nd the servant of the Lord must not strive;
but be gentle unto all men, apt to teach, patient.
2 TIMOTHY 2:24

*F*or we are saved by hope: but hope that is seen
is not hope: for what a man seeth, why doth he
yet hope for? But if we hope for that we see not,
then do we with patience wait for it.
ROMANS 8:24–25

*I*t is good that a man should both hope and
quietly wait for the salvation of the LORD.
LAMENTATIONS 3:26

Rest in the LORD, and wait patiently
for him: fret not thyself because
of him who prospereth in his way,
because of the man who bringeth
wicked devices to pass. Cease from
anger, and forsake wrath: fret not
thyself in any wise to do evil. For
evildoers shall be cut off: but those
that wait upon the LORD, they
shall inherit the earth.

PSALM 37:7–9

Keep thy heart with all diligence;
for out of it are the issues of life.
PROVERBS 4:23

For whatsoever things were written aforetime
were written for our learning, that we through
patience and comfort of the scriptures might
have hope. Now the God of patience and
consolation grant you to be likeminded one
toward another according to Christ Jesus.
ROMANS 15:4–5

The thoughts of the diligent tend
only to plenteousness; but of every one
that is hasty only to want.
PROVERBS 21:5

A time to rend, and a time to sew;
a time to keep silence, and a time to speak.
ECCLESIASTES 3:7

For ye have need of patience, that,
after ye have done the will of God,
ye might receive the promise.
HEBREWS 10:36

Knowing this, that the trying of your faith
worketh patience. But let patience have her
perfect work, that ye may be perfect and entire,
wanting nothing.
JAMES 1:3–4

For what glory is it, if, when ye be buffeted for
your faults, ye shall take it patiently? but if,
when ye do well, and suffer for it, ye take it
patiently, this is acceptable with God.
1 PETER 2:20

Now we exhort you, brethren, warn them
that are unruly, comfort the feebleminded,
support the weak, be patient toward all men.
1 THESSALONIANS 5:14

And the Lord direct your hearts into the love of
God, and into the patient waiting for Christ.
2 Thessalonians 3:5

In your patience possess ye your souls.
Luke 21:19

Better is the end of a thing than the beginning
thereof: and the patient in spirit is better than the
proud in spirit. Be not hasty in thy spirit to be
angry: for anger resteth in the bosom of fools.
Ecclesiastes 7:8–9

I waited patiently for the Lord;
and he inclined unto me, and heard my cry.
Psalm 40:1

Be patient therefore, brethren, unto the coming of the Lord. Behold, the husbandman waiteth for the precious fruit of the earth, and hath long patience for it, until he receive the early and latter rain. Be ye also patient; stablish your hearts: for the coming of the Lord draweth nigh.

JAMES 5:7–8

And therefore will the LORD wait, that he
may be gracious unto you, and therefore will
he be exalted, that he may have mercy upon
you: for the LORD is a God of judgment:
blessed are all they that wait for him.
ISAIAH 30:18

He hath made every thing beautiful in his time:
also he hath set the world in their heart, so
that no man can find out the work that God
maketh from the beginning to the end.
ECCLESIASTES 3:11

Yea, let none that wait on thee be ashamed: let
them be ashamed which transgress without cause.
PSALM 25:3

SEEKING GOD

Has your search for God started to resemble video footage of New Year's Eve from Times Square—unfocused, overwhelming, and full of distraction?

One of the most amazing things about our Savior is that even when we are feeling spiritually and emotionally lost, He's reaching out to us all the time in every way imaginable. Every smile from a stranger, every unexpected visit from a loved one, and every burst of warmth from the hearth is God's way of saying, "Don't despair, I'm here with you."

Make this the year that you discover and acknowledge the Lord's presence in your life and develop an everlasting relationship with Him.

Dear Father, I am humbled by Your efforts to reach me when I'm struggling to find You. Open my eyes to Your presence in my life. Amen.

Yet man is born unto trouble, as the sparks
fly upward. I would seek unto God,
and unto God would I commit my cause.
JOB 5:7–8

And in that day ye shall ask me nothing. Verily,
verily, I say unto you, Whatsoever ye shall ask the
Father in my name, he will give it you. Hitherto
have ye asked nothing in my name: ask, and ye
shall receive, that your joy may be full.
JOHN 16:23–24

But without faith it is impossible to please him:
for he that cometh to God must believe that
he is, and that he is a rewarder of
them that diligently seek him.
HEBREWS 11:6

*B*ut thou, when thou prayest, enter into thy closet, and when thou hast shut thy door, pray to thy Father which is in secret; and thy Father which seeth in secret shall reward thee openly. But when ye pray, use not vain repetitions, as the heathen do: for they think that they shall be heard for their much speaking.

MATTHEW 6:6–7

The Lord is nigh unto all them that call upon
him, to all that call upon him in truth.
Psalm 145:18

The eyes of the Lord are upon the righteous,
and his ears are open unto their cry.
Psalm 34:15

Ask, and it shall be given you; seek, and ye
shall find; knock, and it shall be opened
unto you: for every one that asketh receiveth;
and he that seeketh findeth; and to him that
knocketh it shall be opened.
Matthew 7:7–8

One thing have I desired of the Lord, that will
I seek after; that I may dwell in the house of the
Lord all the days of my life, to behold the beauty
of the Lord, and to enquire in his temple.
Psalm 27:4

Evening, and morning, and at noon, will I pray,
and cry aloud: and he shall hear my voice.
PSALM 55:17

Then shall ye call upon me, and ye shall go and
pray unto me, and I will hearken unto you.
And ye shall seek me, and find me, when ye
shall search for me with all your heart.
JEREMIAH 29:12–13

Blessed are they which do hunger and thirst after
righteousness: for they shall be filled.
MATTHEW 5:6

Casting all your care upon him;
for he careth for you.
1 PETER 5:7

*I*f any of you lack wisdom, let him ask
of God, that giveth to all men liberally, and
upbraideth not; and it shall be given him.
JAMES 1:5

*W*hen the poor and needy seek water,
and there is none, and their tongue faileth
for thirst, I the LORD will hear them,
I the God of Israel will not forsake them.
ISAIAH 41:17

*T*he young lions do lack, and suffer hunger:
but they that seek the LORD shall not
want any good thing.
PSALM 34:10

*A*nd Jesus said unto them, I am the bread of life:
he that cometh to me shall never hunger; and he
that believeth on me shall never thirst.
JOHN 6:35

And all these blessings shall come on thee, and overtake thee, if thou shalt hearken unto the voice of the LORD thy God. Blessed shalt thou be in the city, and blessed shalt thou be in the field. Blessed shall be the fruit of thy body, and the fruit of thy ground, and the fruit of thy cattle, the increase of thy kine, and the flocks of thy sheep. Blessed shall be thy basket and thy store. Blessed shalt thou be when thou comest in, and blessed shalt thou be when thou goest out.

DEUTERONOMY 28:2–6

The eyes of all wait upon thee; and thou givest
them their meat in due season. Thou openest
thine hand, and satisfiest the desire of every
living thing. The LORD is righteous in all
his ways, and holy in all his works.
PSALM 145:15–17

Then shalt thou call, and the LORD shall answer;
thou shalt cry, and he shall say, Here I am.
ISAIAH 58:9

SELF-IMPROVEMENT

It's easy to look in the mirror and see flaws we want to fix on the outside—thighs to tone, wrinkles to erase, and hair to color and recolor. But what about the imperfections that aren't so obvious—the things that slowly damage and disfigure our hearts and minds?

Make it a goal to go before God and ask Him to reveal where you could use some improvement on the inside. Could you work on becoming a better listener? How about trading in a selfish attitude for a spirit of generosity? Everyone may not notice your latest hair color, but a makeover from God definitely has the power to turn heads!

Loving God, thank You for knowing me better than I know myself. Reveal how I can become a better servant to You. Amen.

Do all things without murmurings
and disputings.
Philippians 2:14

Blessed is the man unto whom the
Lord imputeth not iniquity, and in
whose spirit there is no guile.
Psalm 32:2

Withhold not good from them to whom
it is due, when it is in the power of thine
hand to do it. Say not unto thy neighbour,
Go, and come again, and to morrow I
will give; when thou hast it by thee.
Proverbs 3:27–28

*B*ut I say unto you, That ye resist
not evil: but whosoever shall smite
thee on thy right cheek, turn to him
the other also. And if any man will
sue thee at the law, and take away thy
coat, let him have thy cloak also. And
whosoever shall compel thee to go
a mile, go with him twain.

MATTHEW 5:39–41

Take heed to yourselves: If thy brother trespass
against thee, rebuke him; and if he repent, forgive
him. And if he trespass against thee seven times in
a day, and seven times in a day turn again to thee,
saying, I repent; thou shalt forgive him.
Luke 17:3–4

Let him that stole steal no more: but
rather let him labour, working with his
hands the thing which is good, that he
may have to give to him that needeth.
Ephesians 4:28

If thou meet thine enemy's ox or his
ass going astray, thou shalt surely
bring it back to him again.
Exodus 23:4

The way of a fool is right in his own eyes:
but he that hearkeneth unto counsel is wise.
Proverbs 12:15

*T*hou knowest the commandments,
Do not commit adultery, Do not kill, Do not
steal, Do not bear false witness, Defraud not,
Honour thy father and mother.
MARK 10:19

*H*e that is slow to anger is better than the
mighty; and he that ruleth his spirit
than he that taketh a city.
PROVERBS 16:32

*C*onfess your faults one to another, and pray one
for another, that ye may be healed. The effectual
fervent prayer of a righteous man availeth much.
JAMES 5:16

*B*ut above all things, my brethren, swear not,
neither by heaven, neither by the earth, neither
by any other oath: but let your yea be yea; and
your nay, nay; lest ye fall into condemnation.
JAMES 5:12

Let another man praise thee, and not thine own
mouth; a stranger, and not thine own lips.
PROVERBS 27:2

Let us hear the conclusion of the whole matter:
Fear God, and keep his commandments:
for this is the whole duty of man.
ECCLESIASTES 12:13

Say unto wisdom, Thou art my sister;
and call understanding thy kinswoman.
PROVERBS 7:4

No man can serve two masters: for either he
will hate the one, and love the other; or else
he will hold to the one, and despise the other.
Ye cannot serve God and mammon.
MATTHEW 6:24

*F*inally, brethren, whatsoever
things are true, whatsoever things
are honest, whatsoever things
are just, whatsoever things are
pure, whatsoever things are lovely,
whatsoever things are of good report;
if there be any virtue, and if there be
any praise, think on these things.

PHILIPPIANS 4:8

*F*orbearing one another, and forgiving one
another, if any man have a quarrel against any:
even as Christ forgave you, so also do ye.
Colossians 3:13

*W*here there is no vision, the people perish:
but he that keepeth the law, happy is he.
Proverbs 29:18

I know thy works, and charity, and service,
and faith, and thy patience, and thy works;
and the last to be more than the first.
Revelation 2:19

SELF-CONTROL

Irony can be cruel. After all, how are we supposed to embrace an attitude of self-discipline when the holiday season surrounds us with food and family friction? Where's the satisfaction in biting our tongues—but not that second slice of cheesecake?

Self-control isn't easy, but instead of focusing on all the things you're giving up, try focusing on all the positive things you'll gain as a result. Self-discipline can help you build better habits, sustain healthy relationships, and even strengthen your prayer life. God wants us to be examples of his love and compassionate sacrifice, and He has great rewards in store for those who follow His lead.

Lend me Your strength, Lord, as I battle against my weaknesses. I want to become a better person for You. Amen.

He that hath no rule over his own spirit is like
a city that is broken down, and without walls.
Proverbs 25:28

For the drunkard and the glutton shall
come to poverty: and drowsiness
shall clothe a man with rags.
Proverbs 23:21

When wisdom entereth into thine heart, and
knowledge is pleasant unto thy soul; discretion
shall preserve thee, understanding shall keep thee:
To deliver thee from the way of the evil man.
Proverbs 2:10–12

Keep thee from the evil woman, from the flattery of the tongue of a strange woman. Lust not after her beauty in thine heart; neither let her take thee with her eyelids. For by means of a whorish woman a man is brought to a piece of bread: and the adulteress will hunt for the precious life. Can a man take fire in his bosom, and his clothes not be burned? Can one go upon hot coals, and his feet not be burned? So he that goeth in to his neighbour's wife; whosoever toucheth her shall not be innocent.

PROVERBS 6:24–29

Wait on the LORD: be of good courage,
and he shall strengthen thine heart:
wait, I say, on the LORD.
PSALM 27:14

Let us walk honestly, as in the day; not in rioting
and drunkenness, not in chambering and
wantonness, not in strife and envying. But put ye
on the Lord Jesus Christ, and make not provision
for the flesh, to fulfil the lusts thereof.
ROMANS 13:13–14

For in many things we offend all. If any man
offend not in word, the same is a perfect man,
and able also to bridle the whole body.
JAMES 3:2

Wherefore, my beloved brethren, let every man
be swift to hear, slow to speak, slow to wrath.
JAMES 1:19

Let your moderation be known unto all men.
The Lord is at hand.
PHILIPPIANS 4:5

And every man that striveth for the mastery is
temperate in all things. Now they do it to obtain
a corruptible crown; but we an incorruptible.
1 CORINTHIANS 9:25

Hast thou found honey? eat so much
as is sufficient for thee, lest thou be
filled therewith, and vomit it.
PROVERBS 25:16

A fool uttereth all his mind: but a wise
man keepeth it in till afterwards.
PROVERBS 29:11

Be sober, grave, temperate, sound
in faith, in charity, in patience.
TITUS 2:2

Meats for the belly, and the belly for meats: but
God shall destroy both it and them. Now the
body is not for fornication, but for the Lord;
and the Lord for the body. And God hath both
raised up the Lord, and will also raise up us by
his own power. Know ye not that your bodies
are the members of Christ? shall I then take
the members of Christ, and make them the
members of an harlot? God forbid. What? know
ye not that he which is joined to an harlot is
one body? for two, saith he, shall be one flesh.
But he that is joined unto the Lord is one spirit.
Flee fornication. Every sin that a man doeth
is without the body; but he that committeth
fornication sinneth against his own body. What?
know ye not that your body is the temple of the
Holy Ghost which is in you, which ye have of
God, and ye are not your own? For ye are bought
with a price: therefore glorify God in your body,
and in your spirit, which are God's.

1 Corinthians 6:13–20

Be ye angry, and sin not: let not the
sun go down upon your wrath.

Ephesians 4:26

The aged women likewise, that they be in behaviour as becometh holiness, not false accusers, not given to much wine, teachers of good things; that they may teach the young women to be sober, to love their husbands, to love their children, to be discreet, chaste, keepers at home, good, obedient to their own husbands, that the word of God be not blasphemed.

TITUS 2:3–5

Meekness, temperance:
against such there is no law.
GALATIANS 5:23

In like manner also, that women adorn
themselves in modest apparel, with
shamefacedness and sobriety; not with broided
hair, or gold, or pearls, or costly array; but
(which becometh women professing
godliness) with good works.
1 TIMOTHY 2:9–10

Likewise, ye wives, be in subjection to your
own husbands; that, if any obey not the word,
they also may without the word be won by the
conversation of the wives. . . . Whose adorning
let it not be that outward adorning of plaiting
the hair, and of wearing of gold, or of putting on
of apparel; but let it be the hidden man of the
heart, in that which is not corruptible, even the
ornament of a meek and quiet spirit, which
is in the sight of God of great price.
1 PETER 3:1, 3–4

STARTING FRESH

A clean slate equals endless opportunity, and the New Year is a time to celebrate with crisp new calendars and immaculate planner pages.

But that enduring expression, "out with the old and in with the new" doesn't just apply to last year's date book—it's also a great reminder that we must seek God's forgiveness to erase our past sins and make room for bigger and better ambitions—like reconciling the grudges we've been holding or improving a damaged relationship.

So what are you waiting for? Pencil in some time with the Lord and let the transformation begin.

Dear Lord, I'm ready to put the past behind me. Grant me a clean heart and guide me in the year ahead. Amen.

O sing unto the LORD a new song:
sing unto the LORD, all the earth.
PSALM 96:1

Having therefore these promises,
dearly beloved, let us cleanse ourselves
from all filthiness of the flesh and spirit,
perfecting holiness in the fear of God.
2 CORINTHIANS 7:1

Repent ye therefore, and be converted,
that your sins may be blotted out, when
the times of refreshing shall come from
the presence of the Lord.
ACTS 3:19

Thou hast turned for me my mourning into
dancing: thou hast put off my sackcloth, and
girded me with gladness; to the end that my glory
may sing praise to thee, and not be silent. O LORD
my God, I will give thanks unto thee for ever.
PSALM 30:11–12

The Spirit of the Lord GOD is upon me;
because the LORD hath anointed me to preach
good tidings unto the meek; he hath sent me to
bind up the brokenhearted, to proclaim liberty
to the captives, and the opening of the prison to
them that are bound; to proclaim the acceptable
year of the LORD, and the day of vengeance of
our God; to comfort all that mourn.

ISAIAH 61:1–2

Therefore let us keep the feast, not with
old leaven, neither with the leaven of malice
and wickedness; but with the unleavened
bread of sincerity and truth.

1 CORINTHIANS 5:8

No man putteth a piece of new cloth unto an old
garment, for that which is put in to fill it up taketh
from the garment, and the rent is made worse.
Neither do men put new wine into old bottles:
else the bottles break, and the wine runneth out,
and the bottles perish: but they put new wine into
new bottles, and both are preserved.

MATTHEW 9:16–17

Therefore if any man be in Christ,
he is a new creature: old things are passed away;
behold, all things are become new.
2 CORINTHIANS 5:17

And the times of this ignorance God winked at;
but now commandeth all men
every where to repent.
ACTS 17:30

I have blotted out, as a thick cloud,
thy transgressions, and, as a cloud, thy sins:
return unto me; for I have redeemed thee.
ISAIAH 44:22

Create in me a clean heart, O God;
and renew a right spirit within me.
PSALM 51:10

As far as the east is from the west, so far
hath he removed our transgressions from us.
PSALM 103:12

If we confess our sins, he is faithful and just to
forgive us our sins, and to cleanse us from all
unrighteousness.
1 JOHN 1:9

For I will be merciful to their unrighteousness,
and their sins and their iniquities will
I remember no more.
HEBREWS 8:12

Come now, and let us reason together,
saith the LORD: though your sins be as scarlet,
they shall be as white as snow; though they be
red like crimson, they shall be as wool.
ISAIAH 1:18

Turn thou us unto thee, O LORD, and we shall
be turned; renew our days as of old.
LAMENTATIONS 5:21

Blessed be the God and Father of our Lord Jesus
Christ, which according to his abundant mercy
hath begotten us again unto a lively hope by the
resurrection of Jesus Christ from the dead.
1 PETER 1:3

Then will I sprinkle clean water upon you,
and ye shall be clean: from all your filthiness,
and from all your idols, will I cleanse you.
A new heart also will I give you, and a new
spirit will I put within you: and I will take
away the stony heart out of your flesh,
and I will give you an heart of flesh.
EZEKIEL 36:25–26

TEMPTATION

Is that leftover piece of chocolate cake calling to you from the kitchen? Is the sofa looking a whole lot more comfortable than those rigid exercise machines at the gym?

It's so easy to lose sight of our goals in the face of temptation, but luckily we have one of the best role models to gain inspiration and strength from: Jesus! After fasting alone in the desert for forty days, He triumphed over the Devil's enticements and emerged stronger than ever. So don't be afraid to confide in Him and seek His help—no matter what kind of temptation you're facing. He is always there—ready to guide you down the right path.

Father, lead me from temptation as I strive to better myself this year. Your path is the path of righteousness. Amen.

There hath no temptation taken you but such
as is common to man: but God is faithful, who
will not suffer you to be tempted above that ye
are able; but will with the temptation also make a
way to escape, that ye may be able to bear it.

1 Corinthians 10:13

And forgive us our sins; for we also forgive every
one that is indebted to us. And lead us not into
temptation; but deliver us from evil.

Luke 11:4

Brethren, if a man be overtaken in a fault,
ye which are spiritual, restore such an one in
the spirit of meekness; considering thyself,
lest thou also be tempted.

Galatians 6:1

Let love be without dissimulation. Abhor that
which is evil; cleave to that which is good.

Romans 12:9

*Y*e therefore, beloved, seeing ye know
these things before, beware lest ye also,
being led away with the error of the wicked,
fall from your own stedfastness.

2 PETER 3:17

*D*early beloved, I beseech you as strangers
and pilgrims, abstain from fleshly lusts, which
war against the soul; having your conversation
honest among the Gentiles: that, whereas they
speak against you as evildoers, they may by your
good works, which they shall behold, glorify
God in the day of visitation. Submit yourselves
to every ordinance of man for the Lord's sake:
whether it be to the king, as supreme; or unto
governors, as unto them that are sent by him for
the punishment of evildoers, and for the praise
of them that do well. For so is the will of God,
that with well doing ye may put to silence the
ignorance of foolish men: as free, and not using
your liberty for a cloke of maliciousness,
but as the servants of God.

1 PETER 2:11–16

Blessed is the man that endureth temptation:
for when he is tried, he shall receive the
crown of life, which the Lord hath
promised to them that love him.
James 1:12

Because thou hast kept the word of my patience,
I also will keep thee from the hour of temptation,
which shall come upon all the world, to try
them that dwell upon the earth.
Revelation 3:10

Let no man say when he is tempted, I am
tempted of God: for God cannot be tempted
with evil, neither tempteth he any man.
James 1:13

The Lord knoweth how to deliver
the godly out of temptations.
2 Peter 2:9

*B*ut they that will be rich fall into temptation and a snare, and into many foolish and hurtful lusts, which drown men in destruction and perdition. For the love of money is the root of all evil: which while some coveted after, they have erred from the faith, and pierced themselves through with many sorrows.

1 TIMOTHY 6:9–10

Watch and pray, that ye enter not into
temptation: the spirit indeed is willing,
but the flesh is weak.
Matthew 26:41

When wisdom entereth into thine heart,
and knowledge is pleasant unto thy soul;
discretion shall preserve thee, understanding
shall keep thee: to deliver thee from
the way of the evil man.
Proverbs 2:10–12

For in that he himself hath suffered
being tempted, he is able to succour
them that are tempted.
Hebrews 2:18

Put on the whole armour of God, that ye may be
able to stand against the wiles of the devil.
Ephesians 6:11

Submit yourselves therefore to God.
Resist the devil, and he will flee from you.
JAMES 4:7

For all that is in the world, the lust of the flesh,
and the lust of the eyes, and the pride of life,
is not of the Father, but is of the world.
1 JOHN 2:16

My brethren, count it all joy when ye fall into
divers temptations; knowing this, that the trying
of your faith worketh patience. But let patience
have her perfect work, that ye may be perfect
and entire, wanting nothing.
JAMES 1:2–4

Lay hands suddenly on no man, neither be
partaker of other men's sins: keep thyself pure.
1 TIMOTHY 5:22

*T*hen was Jesus led up of the Spirit into the wilderness to be tempted of the devil. And when he had fasted forty days and forty nights, he was afterward an hungred. And when the tempter came to him, he said, If thou be the Son of God, command that these stones be made bread. But he answered and said, It is written, Man shall not live by bread alone, but by every word that proceedeth out of the mouth of God. Then the devil taketh him up into the holy city, and setteth him on a pinnacle of the temple, and saith unto him, If thou be the Son of God, cast thyself down: for it is written, He shall give his angels charge concerning thee: and in their hands they shall bear thee up, lest at any time thou dash thy foot against a stone. Jesus said unto him, it is written again, Thou shalt not tempt the Lord thy God. Again, the devil taketh him up into an exceeding high mountain, and sheweth him all the kingdoms of the world, and the glory of them; and saith unto him, All these things will I give thee, if thou wilt fall down and worship me. Then saith Jesus unto him, Get thee hence, Satan: for it is written, Thou shalt worship the Lord thy God, and him only shalt thou serve. Then the devil leaveth him, and, behold, angels came and ministered unto him.

MATTHEW 4:1–11